PERSIAN
PAINTING

PERSIAN PAINTING

FROM MINIATURES OF THE
XIII.–XVI. CENTURIES

12 COLOUR PLATES

WITH AN INTRODUCTION BY
BASIL GRAY
Officier in charge of Oriental Antiquities
at the British Museum

IRIS BOOKS
OXFORD UNIVERSITY PRESS / NEW YORK, TORONTO

TO THE MEMORY OF
DENNIS KINCAID

THE IRIS BOOKS ARE PRODUCED
under the direction of
DR. H. ZBINDEN (BERNE)
SWITZERLAND

Copyright (plates and text) by IRIS VERLAG BERNE
Printed in Switzerland 1947

Swiss Edition published by IRIS VERLAG, BERNE
Edition for France published by LIBRAIRIE PLON, PARIS

INTRODUCTION

T he Persian school of miniature painting, which is represented in this volume, was remarkably coherent and quick in development. Though not, of course, entirely without ancestors, yet it had to find for itself a new art-form. Such a development is quite unlooked for if we study the art of Persia in the Sasanian period which immediately preceded the Arab conquest in the seventh century A. D. Sasanian art was an instrument of the state. Its finest and most typical expression is to be found in monumental rock-carvings, all of which represent the ruler in heroic measure, either triumphant over his enemies or being invested with power from heaven. The Persians have never been lacking in a love for colour and we have reason to believe that there was then in existence a flourishing school of wall-painting. Though this is only known from its derivatives at Qusayr 'Amra and Samarra, and from the related arts of Bamiyan in Afghanistan and of Qizyl in Turkestan, it must have been an art using illusionistic technique to make a more than natural impression. It was thus parallel both in aim and method with the art of the poster today. There was also a book-art in Persia at this time, namely that employed by the Manichees and referred to by St. Augustine ("Contra Faustum") in a famous passage describing the sumptuous vehicles for the propagation of false doctrine. So far as we can judge from the small fragments of manuscript recovered from Central Asia and now in Berlin, this too was an art of the same kind, delighting in gorgeous colouring but impressive rather than expressive.

In Europe manuscript illumination has served either to illustrate, or to decorate the book. It has been either didactic or decorative, in fact essentially a book art. The same may be said, in a sense, of the Persian miniature, but only because of a rather different attitude to the book itself. Even the most beautiful humanistic hand conforms primarily to the standard of legibility, but Persian calligraphy is more than good writing. And so in the same way the Persian miniature does more than illustrate the text.

For the most part the manuscripts with miniatures are of epics or romantic poems. There is reason to believe that the oldest tradition was in the illustration of the national epic, the *Shahnama* or Book of Kings, in which it is very likely that there was continuity from Sasanian

times, Firdausi, the late tenth century author or redactor of the poem, having crystalized in his work the traditional stories of the Persians about their own history. But, judging from the earliest surviving illustrated copies, which date from the early fourteenth century, this tradition might have died away into insignificance without producing any masterpiece. The miniatures are essentially narrative; figures simply arranged, for the most part on one plane only, against a curtain or conventional background. The dramatic and hieratic qualities here present in high degree, though not absent from the later Persian miniatures, are not their most characteristic qualities. Consequently they have not been drawn on for illustration in this book.

The essential nature of these characteristics and the questions of when and how they developed may best be treated together. A criterion is that the material subject of the painting (usually just one of these well-known scenes from the national legend) has been thoroughly transfused by the imagination. In front of his subject the artist has felt an emotion which has particularised it in this unique presentation. It would not be true to say, exactly, either that he has expressed himself or illustrated the subject, but that the subject has made a deep impression on him, and this unique impression is what he is setting down in order to share it with others. Naturally, for such well-known themes, constantly treated, compositional schemes became established. In Persia it was not regarded a plagiarism to borrow from another's work. The interest was in the emotional handling of the traditional theme.

But even this does not go to the core of the subject. If this were all, or the main part, the general impression of Persian miniatures might be of dramatic scenes of action, treated with a certain hieratic ceremony proper to the subject — in fact the definition which we have given to the early Shahnama illustrations, with an added intensity. What we find however is a tendency to transcend the occasion, so that the action is, at it were, seen with the eye of heaven. Some may suspect in front of these mortal combats on flowery meadows a sentimentalism which would spread a veil of poetical unreality over everything. But consider such a scene as that reproduced on plate 5, the meeting of Humay and Humayun in the garden, where flowers are in fact an essential part of the subject as illustration. What has happened? The flowers are not a background: they are in the forefront of the picture: it is the human figures which are subordinated to the extent of having taken on a flower-like stance in arrested expectancy. Here we are shown the scene of the lovers' meeting as it might have appeared to themselves in recollection. It is, in fact, an imaginative reflection on a sensual experience which the artist has put down. The intensity of presentation suits the occasion, but has a more universal extension.

In another instance, where the scene is the struggle of the faithful horse Rakhsh with a marauding lion to protect his sleeping master Rustam (plate 7), since the only actors are animals, the spectator is almost forced into the position of a supramundane consciousness. The action appears stripped of its temporal character and accidents; and the vigour of the animal combat is matched by the glory of the flowers and trees. There is in European art nothing to compare with this. Rubens treating a similar subject of a lion fight, reaches into a timeless animal world, but the vegetable world is given no prominence. Strength and vitality without glory is the result.

6

To return to our former question, what has happened to make the artist of the classic age of the Persian miniature leave behind the illusionist art of Sasanian Persia with its figures before a curtain? How has the world of nature taken the place of the curtain and engulfed the actors themselves? Several answers have been given—the favourite one that this was due to the revelation of Chinese landscape painting which came to Persia when the Mongol conquest of Chingiz and Qubilay (13th century), united the two ends of Asia. Others would say that this fondness for depicting luxurious vegetation and brilliant flowers is born of a nostalgia natural to the arid soil and burning skies of much of Persia, the same which led to the high estimation of the garden, an intensely cultivated, carefully irrigated plot. Others would seek a deeper explanation in the pantheistic flavour of that mysticism which affected all educational circles in Persia from the tenth century onwards. There is truth in all these suggestions.

The appearance of a school of painting which maintained itself in stability (a movement without changes) for three hundred years, in a way that is unique in the world's history, implies a new psychological attitude, not only in the artist but also in the circles for whom he worked. The explanation can evidently not be found in political history. The period in question opens with Persia divided among a number of states under rulers of different race: it sees the catastrophic invasion of Timur and the establishment of the rule of his house; a new division upon its decline and the Uzbek conquests; and finally the arrival in power of a national Persian dynasty, the Safawi house. The school persisted through all changes without essential loss. Persian civilisation survived.

In the history of Persian poetry the classic period opens with Firdausi about 1000, reaches its height with Nizami (12th) Sa'di (13th) and Hafiz (14th century), and produces its last great poet in Jami (15th century). Though the early illuminated manuscripts have perished, there is enough evidence remaining to make it clear that no style was established before the 14th century. Painting was thus two or three hundred years behind poetry in reestablishing itself after the break in national culture caused by the Arab conquest. This would appear, from the history of the two arts in Europe, to be no isolated phenomenon.

This reflection strengthens, if it is necessary, our view of the existence of a deep cultural movement in Persia which was not thwarted by the unpromising political situation. Writers who have sought, like Professor Edward Browne, to collect biographical information about the Persian poets have lamented the poverty of the material. But it is rich compared with what we have for the painters. That this is not wholly due to their comparatively obscure rank in society may be guessed from the fact that Dawlatshah mentions Khalil, a painter at the court of Shah Rukh (d. 1436) among the four artists who were the pride of Herat at this time. Bihzad, the most famous of all Persian painters, was a familiar and friend of ministers and courtiers in the same city two generations later. But before the late fifteenth century we know the names of only half a dozen other painters and only one of them is represented by a signed painting which has survived. (This is the miniature by Junayd *Naqqash* here reproduced [plate 4]). Its existence is of great importance as corroborating the names given in the few literary sources, and as showing that artists do sometimes sign their work as early as the end of the fourteenth century. Though the evidence is so scanty it seems that we

should not be wrong to think of the progress of the school as in the hands of a very small number of masters who were the ornaments of the courts of the leading rulers of the day, probably consorting on equal terms with poets and learned men and even mixing as did the poets with ministers of state and princes. Patronage was the system supporting all the arts, and the materials of the painter were particularly costly, while his output can never have been large. Consequently the surviving examples, though not numerous, are not to be thought an insignificant remnant of the original. No doubt there were at all times pedestrian craftsmen who copied the masterpieces to which they could get access. The scholar, archeologist or historian may well mourn the great libraries destroyed in the wars of medieval Persia under Samanids, Ghaznawids and Seljuks and above all in the catastrophic Mongol invasions, but it is improbable that the illuminated manuscripts which they contained were of great artistic value.

We can produce no example of the primitive manuscript illumination of Persia. The page from the manuscript of Hariri's *Maqamat*, dated A.D. 1237, now preserved in the Bibliothèque Nationale in Paris (plate 1), shows the style practiced in Baghdad at this date. Baghdad was then still the capital of the Caliphate, a cosmopolitan city. It is therefore not to be considered pure Persian work. Nevertheless the Persian was one of the influences going to make this art of lively, vigorous delineation. The colour scheme is simple and effective, and throughout the whole of this school and age the range of colouring is similarly restricted. It can truly be called decorative, for it is remote from the natural world but nearer to designs applied to glass and pottery. Similar drawing and colouring occur also in Christian manuscripts of about the same period, from the region of Syria. In spite of the expressive and dramatic force of the drawing it shows a lack of tradition and experience. Indeed it may be said to be the work of the heart rather than the head: humourous but simple.

If we turn from this drawing to the products of the Persian school a hundred years later, we are concious of a totally different atmosphere. To an intermediate period belongs a small group of splendid manuscripts produced at the capital of the Il-Khani rulers of Persia, Tabriz. Here in 1295 a new patron appeared when Ghazan Khan mounted the throne. He accepted Islam as the state religion of his country and encouraged learning and the arts. From then until the death of Abu Sa'id in 1335 the Mongol court offered patronage to artists.

From this intermediate period come a number of famous manuscripts which can be securely connected with Tabriz and its neighbourhood and are quite distinct in style from the traditional manuscripts of the *Shahnama* already mentioned and still more so from the school of Baghdad and Mesopotamia. It is therefore just to speak of this as the special Mongol school. In the Pierpont Morgan library at New York is a natural history which contains its earliest examples: divided between London and Edinburgh is all that remains of a history of the world, composed by Rashid al-Din, chief minister to the Mongols, and written and illuminated at his library just outside Tabriz between 1306 and 1314. We have chosen here to represent this school two pages from a famous manuscript of the *Shahnama* (plates 2 and 3). Though no colophon is known, it is now generally agreed that it mus have been prepared at Tabriz about 1330. It seems to have contained between fifty and

eighty miniatures, most of which are now in museums and private collections in America. In these for the first time is to be seen the unique relation of figures and landscape which is to persist throughout the rest of the history of Persian painting. Often (and of this plate 2 is an excellent example) the source of the landscape element is at once apparent. The tree in this picture is directly derived from a Chinese landscape painting. But the artist has used it as an essential element in his composition. It is no symbol of landscape, no conventional background. On the contrary it gives scale and importance to the human figures in front of it, while not only does its thrusting growth from left to right carry the eye in this direction so as to rest on the captive King, but it bends back to provide a crown of greenery for his conqueror, the new ruler. If a number of these miniatures are studied it will be seen that this is no fanciful reconstruction or accidental manner, but a clear instance of the dramatic use of the whole content of the painting to focus attention and to evoke one clear emotion. The mastery of landscape painting has enormously enriched the power of the artist to do this. He has now as it were an orchestra instead of the human voice alone.

After 1335 local rulers took the place of a united government. After the middle of the fourteenth century two houses carved out for themselves large dominions, the Jala'ir house, who were related to the Mongol Il-Khans, ruled at Baghdad and Tabriz, the Muzzaffarids, a Persian family from Khurasan, had Shiraz for their capital. But neither the race of the patron nor the locality seems to have influenced the development of the classical school of Persian painting, for there is nothing to differentiate the art of Baghdad from that of Shiraz at the end of the fourteenth century.

It was at this time that what is known as the Timurid style was formed, actually not in the first place at the court of Timur himself, whose invasions caused such widespread ruin that the beneficent rule of his family in the succeeding two generations could not repair the damage. But while the conqueror from the steppe, was marching through the land, in Fars and in Iraq and Azarbaijan, Persian miniature painting was painfully finding its way to what was to be its classic style. At first it was halting and crude, showing a great lapse from the Mongol school of about 1330 to this new style which may have been inaugurated about 1370, after a period from which we have virtually nothing. But it quickly reached fruition apparently simultaneously at Baghdad (as exemplified in the Diwan of Khwaju Kirmani from which comes our plate 4) and at Shiraz in a volume of epics now divided between the British Museum and the Chester Beatty collection. The date of both these is 1397. Within a generation this school was producing at Herat and Shiraz a succession of assured masterpieces. Though greater triumphs of individual artists were to come later, the general standard of Persian painting was never higher. It seems as though the artists were all filled with an unflagging enthusiasm by the discovery of this new means of expression. It has been difficult to choose from among all the products of the school the two or three for which there is room among these reproductions. I regret, particularly, that it has not been possible to include one of the pages from an animal fable book which is preserved in the Gulistan Museum in Teheran and made so deep an impression at the time of the London Exhibition of 1931. But a similar intimate gentleness of sensibility leads the onlooker into

9

the glory of nature in the miniatures we have actually chosen for plates 5, 6 and 7. While the stronger constructive power and tauter composition of the first two is more characteristic of the Timurid school, the last exceeds them in richness and romantic suggestion.

We have spoken of an established, classic, Persian style. What are its special qualities? Its most striking and peculiar gift is its use of colour. The colours are of singular purity, mostly prepared from metallic bases, and are applied flat. It is natural that an art which did not concern itself with temporal relations should not have been interested in spatial illusion. But the art of combination of different colours is of extreme importance. They are used not in a tonal scheme, as in most western painting, but as a chord; they do not foil one another but sing together. They have a positive value in themselves, so that as in Venetian painting a pleasure is to be got from the pigments rendering textures of stuff, so a sensual pleasure is to be had in some colours of the Persian palettes. But here we do not rest in this sensual response: the deep blue above the garden of Humay, the vibrating blue background of the scene in paradise from the *Mi'rajnama* (plate 6) convey the infinite more intensely than any European painter, even Piero della Francesca has ever done. The coats of the horses in Bihzad's *King Dara and the herdsman* (plate 8) are so combined into a bouquet that the impression produced haunts the imagination. The flocks of Samuel Palmer or Calvert are not more vividly put before the imaginative eye. It has been suggested that this raising of everything to its highest pitch is no more than romanticism: but that is to introduce a secondary, human emotion into what is for the Persian no more (nor less) than a statement of cosmic reality. The painter must needs use every resource at his command to depict the smallest flower, if he holds that it is as important, as worthy of attention, as a tree, since God is equally in each. Such a pantheistic view must be understood in order to appreciate rightly the extraordinary care *de minimis*, of the least detail, in Persian miniatures. This is no idle display of skill, no childish trick; it is the result of a natural humility of a man in face of reality and a vindication of artistic integrity of vision. No true artist would of purpose exclude anything which he sees.

We have already spoken of the subjects portrayed in the miniatures in their relation to the poems transcribed in the text of the volumes which contain them. We have seen that the same subjects are treated over and over again. Since, in the eyes of Islam, representational art is a sin, the art of the painter was not called to the aid of religion. The Persian painters never had any message to give but their own. This combination of a school, having the advantage of accepted and traditional subjects well known through the land but free from dogmatic burden, seems to be unique. Two of the miniatures here reproduced do in fact show Muhammad but they show him as a historic person—the Prophet of God; and it should be remembered that to the faithful he is no more than this. The journey of Muhammad on Buraq through the sky (plate 12) is no more a religious subject than any of the others selected. If this painting has a religious flavour it is due to the artist and not to his subject.

BASIL GRAY

10

LIST OF PLATES

WITH NOTES BY BASIL GRAY

The measurements given are of the originals without margin or text.

1. ABU ZAYD AND AL-HARIS QUESTIONING A VILLAGER

Page (folio 138) from a manuscript of the MAQAMAT (Assemblies) of Hariri copied and illustrated by Yahya b. Mahmud b. Yahya b. Abi'l-Hasan b. Kuwwariha al-Wasiti (of Wasit in Mesopotamia) in 634 H. (A. D. 1237).
Bibliothèque Nationale, Paris, Arab. 5847: from the Schefer Collection.—30/23 cm.
Abu Zayd, the hero of the book and al-Haris the narrator, are seen mounted on camels in the foreground.

Behind them (i. e. at the top of the page) is a village in which various shops can be seen while a mosque with minaret rises behind. On the right is a goatherd spinning beside the goats. In the centre is a pool, represented by the swirling convention usually employed for water at this period.—The ninety-nine miniatures contained in this manuscript are the finest work of the Mesopotamian or Baghdad school of the thirteenth century.

2. ARDAWAN BROUGHT BEFORE ARDASHIR

An illustration to the SHAHNAMA of Firdausi, separated from a manuscript which has been dispersed throughout the world since it was on the market in 1912. Probably painted at Tabriz about 1330.
Collection of M. Henri Vever, Paris.—20/29 cm.
In battle against Ardashir, Ardawan is taken prisoner, brought before Ardashir and put to death. In the minia-

ture the executioner is about to carry out the sentence just pronounced. Ardawan (Artabanus) was the last Parthian king: Ardashir, son of Sasan, a herdsman but of royal descent, and the daughter of Papak, prince of Fars, was the founder of the great Sasanian dynasty. (See Mohl, V, p. 241.)

3. FARIDUN RECEIVES THE HEAD OF HIS MURDERED SON IRAJ, BROUGHT TO HIM BY A MESSENGER ON A CAMEL, ALL THE COURTIERS WEEP

A miniature from the same manuscript of the SHAHNAMA as 2. — Tabriz, about 1330.
Collection of M. Henri Vever, Paris.—22/28,5 cm.
Firdausi's poem, the SHAHNAMA or Book of Kings, was finished in 1010 A. D. It is an immensely long epic containing a recension of the Persian tradition of their own history. It opens with accounts of the reigns

of kings of two mythical dynasties, the Pishdadi and the Kayani. Faridun, the first of the Kayanid house, freed the world from the tyrannous rule of the Snake king Zahhak. He had three sons Sam, Tur and Iraj to whom he distributed his vast dominions. The two elder brothers attacked Iraj who had received Iran, out of jealousy and killed him. (See Mohl, I, p. 122.)

4. WEDDING CELEBRATIONS OF PRINCE HUMAY AND PRINCESS HUMAYUN

By Junayd Naqqash Sultani.
Page from a manuscript of the Diwan of Khwaju Kirmani in the *British Museum* (Add. 18113), copied at Baghdad in 798/1396 by Mir 'Ali Tabrizi.— 29,7/19,3 cm.
This manuscript was copied at Baghdad while it was still in the possession of the Jala'ir sultan Ahmad and before its capture by Timur. The scribe Mir 'Ali of Tabriz was the most famous in his day. The artist whose signature is to be found on the window above

the dais in the centre of the composition was also very well-known. Dust Muhammad, writing in 1544, mentions him as an artist of Baghdad, the pupil of Ustad Shams al-Din, court painter of Sultan Uways Jala'ir. 'Abdul-Hayy another pupil of Shams al-Din seems to have been even more highly esteemed.—The miniature here reproduced is the earliest signed Persian miniature known and the only signed work of Junayd, who may however be considered the artist of the other eight miniatures in this manuscript.

5. THE FIRST MEETING OF THE IRANIAN PRINCE HUMAY AND HUMAYUN DAUGHTER OF THE KHAQAN OF CHINA

A page detached from an unknown manuscript containing the mathnawi of Khwaju Kirmani, HUMAY AND HUMAYUN, which was composed at Baghdad in 732 H. (A. D. 1330). The miniature may be attributed to the years 1420-5 and probably belongs to the early school of Herat. It has been suggested by Dr. Kühnel that it may be by the painter Mirza Ghiyas al-Din,

who accompanied Shah Rukh's embassy to China in 1420—23. But it shows no evidence of the artist having actually visited China.
Musée des Arts décoratifs, Paris. — 29/17,5 cm.
Humay was led to seek Humayun in the far east by dreams in which she appeared to him and charmed his heart with her beauty.

6. MUHAMMAD'S VISIT TO PARADISE

A miniature from a manuscript of the MI'RAJ-NAMA or account of the ascension of Muhammad, copied in Eastern Turki (Uighur) script at Herat by Malik Bakhshi in 840 H./1436 A. D.
Bibliothèque Nationale, Paris (Sup. Turc 190). From the collection of Gallard, translator of the THOUSAND AND ONE NIGHTS, who acquired it in Constantinople in 1672.—19,7/16 cm.
In a dream the Prophet was conveyed through the Seven Heavens—and this tradition was elaborated in later treatment of the subject. In a single night mounted on

the human headed steed Buraq (guided by the Archangel Gabriel) he visited the realms of heaven and hell. He is here hovering on his miraculous steed over the fields of paradise in which, it being Friday, the Islamic holiday, the *huris* are paying visits to one another and exchanging nosegays of flowers. Visible " glory " in the form of halo or mandala was probably first represented in Iranian lands. Very often (as in our plate) the face of a holy personage was concealed by it or by a curtain, since Islamic custom wished to avoid any chance of iconolatry.

7. RUSTAM SLEEPING. HIS HORSE RAKHSH PROTECTS HIS MASTER FROM A LION AND DEFEATS IT

A miniature detached from an unknown manuscript of the SHAHNAMA. With two other miniatures from the same manuscript now in the Leipzig museum it was formerly bound up in a copy of the Khamsa of Nizami owned by Ph. W. Schulz. All three are reproduced in his book. The manuscript was apparently never completed, for these miniatures have never had the marginal lines drawn.
Collection of Sir Bernard Eckstein, Bart, Oldlands Hall, *Uckfield.*—31,8/20,8 cm.
The incident illustrated is Rustam's first adventure on going out into the world, as a hero to combat Ahriman the spirit of evil. At the end of a long day's ride he lay

down to rest in an attractive thicket, which was the lair of a lion. The lion returned after the first watch and thought to devour horse and rider. But Rakhsh, Rustam's miraculous horse whom he had chosen from the herds and snatched from his mare, protected him. This scene was a favourite one with the miniaturists who illustrated the SHAHNAMA. (See Mohl, I, p. 404 et seq.) These miniatures stand rather apart from the main stream of Timurid painting. They do not appear to belong to the school of Herat, but cannot be attributed to any other particular centre. Unless the style is very archaic the date can hardly be later than 1475.

8. THE HERDSMAN AND KING DARA

By Bihzad.
A page from a manuscript of the BUSTAN of Sadi copied in 893 H. (1488 A. D.) by Sultan 'Ali al-Katib for Sultan Husayn Mirza, last Timurid ruler of Herat. This manuscript contains five miniatures, four signed by Bihzad in a convincing way and all doubtless by him. They are almost the only work which is admitted by all critics to be autograph. The signature of the present miniature is on the black quiver worn by the King "'AMAL AL-'ABD BIHZAD " (the work of the slave Bihzad). — See Binyon, Wilkinson and Gray, *Persian Miniature Painting*, pls. LXVIII-LXXI and *Burlington Magazine*, Feb. 1931.

Bibliothèque Egyptienne, Cairo.—21,2/16 cm.
The BUSTAN, published in A. D. 1257, is one of the classics of the Persian language. It is a long didactic poem in mathnawi form and the scene treated in the present miniature carries a moral. King Dara (Darius) while out hunting comes upon a herdsman with tha horses in his charge. Not recognising him as his own man the king draws his bow at the stranger. The herdsman then discloses his identity and lectures the king on the ignorance he has shown of his subjects' very existence, giving thus signs of culpable general neglect.

9. PORTRAIT OF A YOUNG PRINCE

Early Safawi school: 1525-1550.
Collection of M. Henri Vever, Paris. — 15,5/12,8 cm.
It was only at the very end of the fifteenth century that it became the practice in Persia to paint separate miniatures not for inclusion in manuscripts though they might afterwards be mounted in an album. At first these were mostly portraits. It has been suggested that the subject of the present miniature was Shah Tahmasp himself, but this is unlikely. He is represented as holding a book in which are written poems in praise of his beauty. He wears the high turban with long stick (*kulah*) which was the headdress introduced by the Safawi house. The feathers in it mark his princely rank.

This miniature may be attributed to the Sayyid Mir Musawwir, who was specially esteemed as a portrait painter and succeeded Bihzad as head of Tahmasp's library staff. A signed painting by him at the British Museum represents a standing figure, painted in closely similar style but on a rather larger scale.

10. THE FALCONER

About 1570 — *Collection of Sir Bernard Eckstein, Bart., Uckfield*, Sussex. — 16,8/10 cm.
The Falconer is evidently a man of rank. In Persia as in Europe hawking was the sport of kings and nobles. Sir John Chardin who visited Persia in the second half of the seventeenth century records how he saw the grandees caressing the falcons which they kept constantly on their fist and decorated with pearls and gold. Here the falcon is jessed with gold cords. There are several well-known treatises on falconry in Persian, one of which was translated into English by Lt. Col. D. C. Phillott from the Baz-Nama-Yi Nasiri.

11. KHUSRAU SEES SHIRIN BATHING IN A POOL

By Sultan Muhammad.
A page from a manuscript of the KHAMSA (Five Poems) of Nizami, copied in 1539-43 by Shah Mahmud Nishapuri at Tabriz for Shah Tahmasp, second ruler of the Safawi line.
British Museum (Or. 2265), *London.* — 29,6/19 cm.
The romantic poem of KHUSRAU AND SHIRIN was composed in 1175 A. D. It recounts the adventures of the Sasanian king Khusrau Parwiz and especially his love for Shirin, a princess of Armenia. Though he has heard tell of her beauty from the painter Shapur, Khusrau first sees her without knowing who she is while she is bathing in a pool as she journeys to Persia. He is bewildered by her beauty. Beside the pool is her famous black horse Shabdiz, faster than any in the world. At first Shirin is unaware of the young man gazing at her. She is filled with confusion when she notices him and he seeing it withdrew. She gathers together her clothes, jumps on her horse and gallops away.

Sultan Muhammad, if not a direct pupil of Bihzad, at least shows himself a successor of his school. But he worked not at Herat but at the new Safawi capital Tabriz. He was one of the foremost painters of the day. Writing in 1544, the year after the completion of the present manuscript, Dust Muhammad calls him the zenith of the age. Delighting in luxuriance of vegetation and richness of detail, he may be seen, in the few works still surviving, to have developed dynamic compositions. He carries further the movement introduced into Persian miniatures by Bihzad.

12. THE PROPHET MUHAMMAD RIDING ON BURAQ THROUGH THE NIGHT SKY ON HIS WAY TO VISIT HEAVEN AND HELL

Though originally considered a dream or vision this journey of Muhammad afterwards came to be considered an actual experience. It was still however confined to a single night.
British Museum (Or. 2265), *London.* — 30/19,5 cm.
The present miniature is from the same manuscript of the KHAMSA of Nizami as the last. It illustrates an introductory dedication to the Creator prefixed by the poet to the Haft Paykar. The Prophet is attended by a host of angels offering him clothes and food, or burning incense and swinging a censer. Preceeding him is the archangel Gabriel while in the distance below him can be seen the dim shape of this earth. — This miniature too was attributed by Mr. Binyon to Sultan Muhammad. It certainly has the two qualities of his work mentioned above, and it is by the hand of a master. Agha Mirak, the other leading painter of the day, executed five miniatures in this manuscript. They show a tendency to concentrate the weight of the composition well inside the borders, as if the artist were a little afraid of the new development in Persian miniatures of open space. Sultan Muhammad is never afraid nor limited in this way.

The twelve plates have been made from new reproductions taken directly from the originals. They are printed in ten-colour process by the IRIS PRESS, Berne. The selection of subjects was made by Dr. HANS ZBINDEN with the advice of Mr. BASIL GRAY and M. IVAN STCHOUKINE.-The author and editor express their thanks to the Trustees of the British Museum; the Director of the Musée des Arts Décoratifs, Paris; the Bibliothèque Nationale, Paris; the Bibliothèque Egyptienne, Cairo; and to Sir Bernard Eckstein, Bart., Uckfield, and M. Henri Vever, Paris, for kindly permitting the reproduction of miniatures in their collections.—They are also obliged to the Oxford University Press for kindly lending the colour separations of plate 8.
Since the ordinary process of gold-printing is quite incapable of rendering the delicacy, richness and patina of the gold-painting of the originals, it has been thought preferable, in these reproductions, to employ combinations of colour-printing, which give a result nearer to the effect of the gold as it appears in the miniatures.

PLATES

1

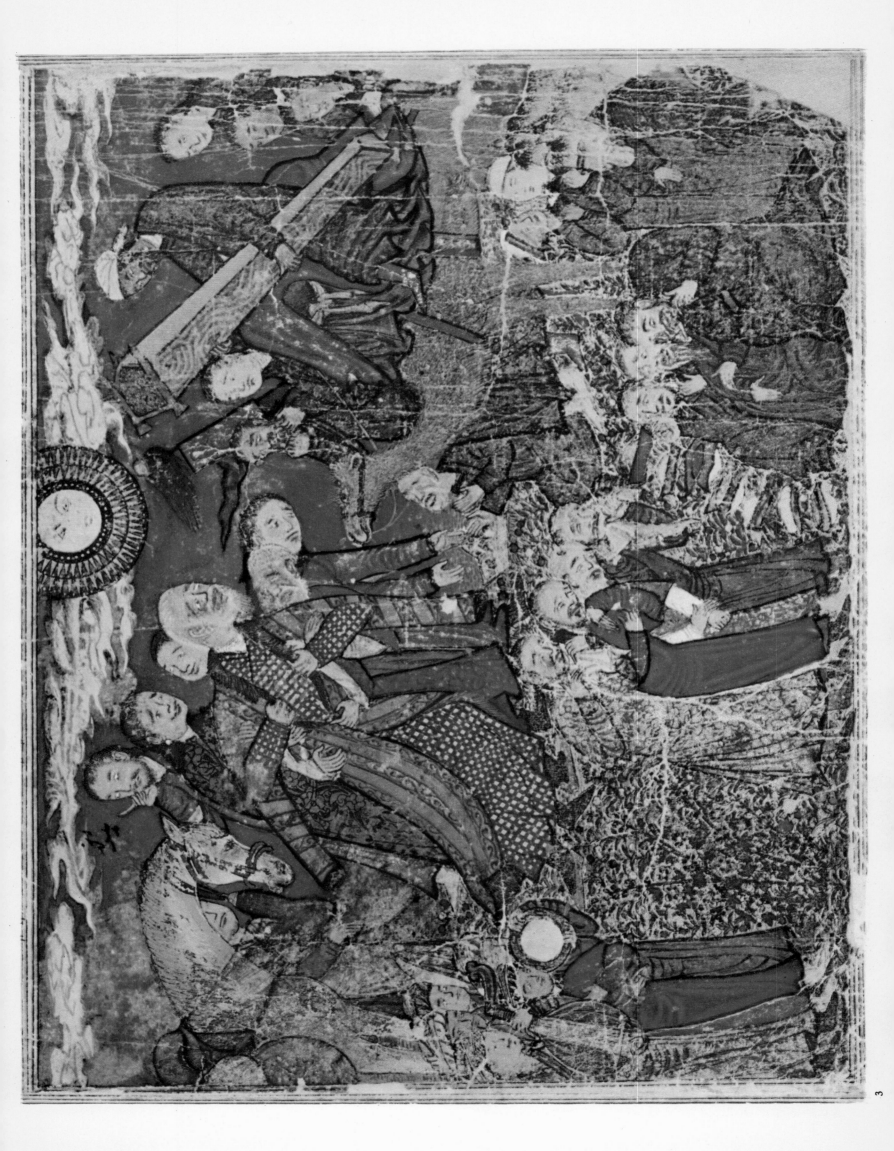

4

9

10

Printed in Switzerland